DIGGING DEEPER

FAITH

PASTORAL
HEALTH CARE
MINISTRY

*"Search the
Scripture"*
—John 5:39

DIGGING
DEEPER
PART 1

DIGGING DEEPER

FAITH

JOHN F. GILLETTE

Author of Pastoral Health Care Series

Chapbook Press

Schuler Books
2660 28th Street SE
Grand Rapids MI 49512

www.schulerbooks.com/chapbook-press

Digging Deeper Book Series Part One
Digging Deeper: Faith
Copyright ©2025 — John F. Gillette. All rights reserved. Published 2023.

Printed at Schuler Books, Chapbook Press, Grand Rapids, Michigan, in the United States of America.

Distribution contact:at jgillette@comcast.net.

ISBN 13: 9781966196549

Library of Congress Control Number: 2025927595

Cover Design: Frank Gutbrod Graphic Design

Printed in the United States of America

Dr. John F Gillette's story started with a miracle, he was born a member of a trio-triplets. He has learned every moment needs to be in God's presence. His desire is to glorify the Lord Jesus Christ in health and in sickness.

A miracle in observing and obeying God's perspective on eternal values. John has developed understanding, compassion, and sovereignty. The proclamation of the sacred scripture has motivated music, ministry, and mentoring. He is a servant of Jesus Christ in the pastoral health care ministry.

Table of Contents

The Testimony of Faith

he songwriter has written, "Come every soul by sin oppressed, there's mercy with the Lord; and he shall surely give you rest by trusting in His word. Only Trust Him, Only Trust Him, He will save you." He will give you rest. Have you read Jesus' words, "Come unto me" in Matthew 11:28-30? Have you heard His sweet, deep, sensitive, authentic, bold, eternal, and changing words?

"Come unto me" is an open invitation. Let's discover what Jesus means with

1

such awesome words. We better start with a little background. The Gospel according to Matthew gives a view of the life of Jesus. Most likely, the early accounts were passed on verbally in the Aramaic language and then recorded in Greek manuscripts dating from A.D.60 to A.D. 90. Matthew emphasizes the Old Testament preparation from the gospel and makes it an ideal "bridge" from the Old to the New Testament. Matthew, the Hebrew tax collector, writes for the Hebrew mind. He tells us that Jesus is the Messiah foretold by the Old Testament prophets. He starts with the genealogy of Jesus. The coming of Christ to the earth has been anticipated from the beginning. In the early days of human history, God chose one family line, that of Abraham, and later on another family with the Abrahamic family, that of David, to be the family through which His son would make entrance into the world.

Miracles, lessons learned and many activities have already taken place, but now we have come to chapter eleven of Matthew, verse 28-30, to think about Jesus' sweet words "Come unto me." The purpose of the gospel is to present the good news of the Redeemer-Savior. Jesus is the Messiah of Israel, the Son of God, and the Savior of the Word.

"Come unto me" are life-changing words but they can't be heard by our sinful, rebellious and stubborn minds without a sovereignly bestowed spiritual awakening. We read of a free offer to all in verses 28-30 and a divine initiative in verse 27. I'm so glad that the Holy Spirit convicts us and the sovereign work of God is a hand so that we can trust our spirit, soul and body to Jesus Christ.

Authority and confidence are found in verse 27."All things are delivered unto me of my father: and no man knoweth the Son, but the Father: neither knoweth any man the Father save the Son,and he to whomsoever the Son will reveal Him." Jesus is the way initiated by the Father. "My Father" reveals Jesus' absolute equality; He is the "only begotten Son." Personal knowledge of the Holy Spirit will develop assurance and authority in living. How does genuine conversion take place? The songwriter says, "Only Trust Him" and the text continues with the answer.

"All ye that labor and are heavy laden" are words that describe our condition. If we are going to hear God's call through Jesus, we have to be in a condition of humility. The labour and burden has brought us to exhaustion and just plain sweat. We have to lay our load at Jesus' feet. To save ourselves will not work, doing all the good work will not do it, a guilty conscience will not do it, but a broken heart realizing total dependence is necessary. We will hear his voice "Come unto me" when we recognize our sinful condition. In the present condition we don't measure up to God's standards. In my childhood, I responded to Jesus. I had been singing with my sisters at a Bible Conference. On the way home, our mother asked if we would like to ask Jesus into our hearts. We knew the gospel story. Because of sin, we were separated from God (Rom. 3:23), and the penalty for sin in death (Rom. 6:23). Thankfully that penalty for sin was paid by Jesus Christ (Rom. 5:8). If we repent of the sin (Acknowledge need), then confess and trust Jesus as Lord Savior (accept Jesus), we will be saved (Rom. 10:9). Right there in the car by the side of the road, I was "born of God" and a second birth (spiritual) took place (I John 5:11-12). This birth is clearly stated in John 3:8, "The wind bloweth where it listeth, and thou hearst the sound thereof, but cannot tell whence it cometh, and whither it goeth: so is everyone that is born of the Spirit." The wind, which is the same word used for Spirit, cannot be seen or explained. The word can only be heard or observed in relation to its effect. The new birth is spiritual and invisible. One can only observe the results. It's a decision of faith based upon facts. The first element in trusting Jesus is total dependency.

"And I will give you rest… ye shall find rest unto your souls" are powerful words. It's not only a dependent heart that is necessary but the discovery of divine truth found in Jesus Christ who provides the rest for our souls. Liberation is given through Jesus. We can entrust our spirit, soul, and body to Jesus because of who He is. In the Gospel of John, Jesus is revealed as the eternal, pre-existing Son of God, who became man in order to reveal the Father and bring eternal life through his death and resurrection. John says, "now Jesus did many other signs in the presence of His disciples, which are not written in this book; but these are written that you may believe that Jesus is the Christ, the Son of God, and that believing you may have life in His name" (John 20:30-31).

Jesus is God. "In the beginning was the Word, and the Word was with God, and the Word was God. He was in the beginning with God." In John 1:14 it says, "the Word became flesh." The key term,

Word, refers to Jesus. Jesus is fully God. These phrases are vital to understand. "In the beginning" refers to eternity past. It goes beyond his earthy life, beyond even the beginning of creation into eternity. "With God" refers to an affirmation of Christ's separate personality. The diversity within the Godhead. "And God was the Word" refers to the fact that Jesus is fully divine in all respects. We can trust Jesus because He is God. He has the authority and power to redeem us and bring us into his family to faith.

"Take my yoke upon you and learn of me; for I am meek and lowly in heart" are words of challenge and life- changeling possibilities. We must turn around in our thinking. We must turn to Jesus and repent. Our way to acceptance and forgiveness is not acceptable. A complete turnaround and a full change of direction are necessary. We have come to the end of our resources. As we learn of Him, we discover our self-regulations. Work-based convictions will not be sufficient. He is gentle and tender and is calling us to Himself. As we turn from our sin and replace it with faith, a new direction takes place. This is not an intellectual exercise but a whole heart change.

"For my yoke is easy and my burden is light" are words that remind us that salvation is Jesus Christ includes an invitation to surrender. If we want His saving rest, we must take His yoke. The yoke is a symbol of submission. It is used by the master to direct us. Discipline is a natural result of conversation. The yoke is submission to Christ and is not grievous. It is joyous.

My childhood song to live by tells it all, "I have been chosen by the Father, purchased by the Son, sealed by the Spirit, I'm His very Own" (Eph. 1). As a child, I did not understand everything and I do not even now. His grace is amazing and His sovereignty is above us. All He wants me to do is take him at His word. He said, "By one man (Adam), sin entered into the world and death by sin, and so death passed upon all men for all have sinned" (Rom. 5:12). "Behold I was shaped in iniquity" (Ps. 51:5). I do not like reading these words but God said it and I have to accept it. I have discovered that "ye have chosen me" (John 15:16). "It is God who worketh in you both to will and to do of His good pleasure" (Phil. 2:13). He is drawing me to Himself (John 6:44). He has saved me and called me according to His own purpose and grace (II Tim. 1:9).

CHAPTER ONE

What is Faith?

aith is a positive expressive experience based on complete, confident, spiritual insight. Triumph and defeat have generated belief, trust, and faith. I was invited into a relationship with Jesus Christ in my childhood. Faith is the root of the subject. I have been blessed by the supreme Being who is God.

The Bible says, "Whatsoever is born of God, over cometh the world and this is the victory that over cometh the world faith" (I John 5:4). This is a definite turning away from the world. It is setting "eternity in the heart" (Ecc. 3:11). The key word is faith. It is a daily decision to respond to God's word in the correct way. Through faith I have been forgiven, the Holy Spirit has opened my eyes to the light from the power of satan and has given me faith (Acts 26:8). Forgiveness has provided a relation which justified me through faith (ROm. 6:17, 5:11). God indwells me (Gal. 2:20). Faith has its foundation in the character of the one I believe. It is faith through grace that has imputed righteousness in me (Rom. 4:17-18). It goes back to the first phrase of the introduction. Faith is based upon Jesus Christ who is God (John 1:1-2).

I have seen His sovereign grace at work. He saved me not by works of righteousness that I have done but according to His mercy by the working of regeneration and renewing by the

Holy Spirit (Titus 3:5). I live everyday knowing in whom I have believed and I am persuaded that He is able to keep that to which I have committed on to Him against that day (II Thimothy 1:12). Salvation is of the Lord. I am save because the Father has chosen me, the Son has purchased me, the Holy Spirit has sealed me. Salvation occurs when God changes the Heart and unbeliever turn from sin to Christ (Colossians 1:13). Faith is a process of Jesus to enter the heart and to dwell there (Ephesians 3:17).

Personal Response

CHAPTER TWO

What are the essentials of faith?

aith requires belief and willingness to act based on that belief. Faith is a gift for the non-Christian. The Bible says, faith cometh by hearing the word of God" (Rom. 10:17). Let the word of God (Bible) talk to you. "Look unto Jesus the author and finisher of our faith" (Heb. 12:2). We must decide to hear his call and hear the father draw you to him (John 6:44).

Faith requires repentance. God gives it through grace. It is not emotional awareness but the understanding of self. The Bible says, "I live by faith of the Son of God, who loved me and gave himself for me" (Gal 2:20). Jesus Christ has provided the ability to respond to God.

Faith requires trust of one person in another person. It is a growing process and requires reliance. The Bible says, "believe on the Lord Jesus Christ, and thou shalt be saved" (Act 16:31). Belief starts the path in God's grace. Study about Jesus Christ, it will mature us.

Personal Response

CHAPTER THREE

What is the basis of faith?

The basis of faith is inspiration. "All scripture is given by inspiration of God and is profitable for doctrine, for reproof, for correction, for instruction in righteousness that the man of God may be perfect, through furnishing unto all good works" (II Tim. 3:16,17). Biblical inspiration is the holySpirit guiding human writers and organically unites Himself. God has revealed Himself to us. The word of God is truth. The Holy Spirit enables us to understand. The word of God explains the word trust and obey.

The basis of faith is transformation. It is an inner change of character and nature by the power of God. Man discovers that the Bible is not human but the breathing out of God. It is his product. God has spoken to give us the Bible, but also that he continue to speak through it to individuals. Truth is planted in us by divine influence. There is a direct encounter of the individual delivered with God. The conscience has been taken captive by the word of God. The Bible is infallible, infinite, and authentic.

The basis of faith is conciliation. The word is building you up. Vitality in life comes through faith as its basis.

God's word gives us life. (Phil. 2:16)

God's word can make us righteous (I Cor. 15:1-2)

God's word can produce growth. (I Peter 1:19-20).

God's word sanctifies us (John 17:17).
God's word gives us wisdom.
Ps. 1:19-20)

Personal Response

CHAPTER FOUR

What is the object of faith?

The object of faith is a person. It is God. The creator of all things, infinite in wisdom, power, truth, love, and holiness. He is worthy of all our trust and devotion. God is the object of our faith because of His divine character. He's the eternal, infinite, perfection of love. God said, "I have loved thee with an everlasting love. Therefore, with loving kindness have I drawn thee" (Jer. 31:33). All of His plans and actions are the expression of HIs loving kindness. He has our best interest in mind and delights in our happiness.

He is the external infinite perfection of truth. What he says to us is His word is truth. His actions are always in harmony with His person and word. He is fully trustworthy. He never makes mistakes. He never fails.

He is love. He is truth. He is holy. He says, "you shall be holy, for I am holy". All forms of sin are under His authority and judgment. We can trust God because everything about Him is characterized by holiness.

Personal Response

CHAPTER FIVE

What is the meaning of faith?

aith is not in faith but in God. It is a spiritual, personal relationship with Jesus Christ. The Bible says, "let not your heart be troubled, ye believe in God, believe also in me" (John 14:1). A great tragedy was about to happen. In this desperate moment Jesus asked them to trust Him.

The Bible says, "believe one the Lord Jesus Christ and thou shall be saved and thy house"(Acts 16:11). Biblical faith is not to believe in a thing but in a person.

Involvement is a personal walk with God.

True faith is not faith in faith but in God. "Jesus said to him, I am the resurrection and the life, he that believes in me though he were dead, ye shall he live" (John 11:25). The scripture deals with Lazarus, Martha, and Mary. Faith requires belief in a doctrine (resurrection) and in Jesus Christ. Faith is being united with a sovereign God.

True faith has its source of strength in God. The Bible says, "through faith Sarah received strength to conceive" (Heb.11:14). Faith is action in belief. Faith is a product of God's indwelling.

True faith opens the door to divine peace. The Bible says, "faith effectively worketh in you that believe" (I Thes. 2:13). When a believer wants the will of God, and is willing to obey and live in faith, then God can begin to work in his life.

True faith is connected to knowledge. The Bible says, "faith cometh by hearing" (Rom. 10:17). We must always keep in mind this knowledge can be modified with reason, emotion, desire, and deception. The Bible has to be the authority. Faith is not faith in faith but in God.

Personal Response

CHAPTER SIX

What is the evidence of faith?

ife in Jesus Christ is an affirmation of faith. I sincerely receive the Holy Spirit and my anointing for every part of life and service. "Jesus stood and said in a loud voice, 'If anyone is thirsty, let him come to me and drink. Whoever believes in me, as the scripture has saif, streams of living water will flow from within him" (John 7:31-38).

- My life in Jesus Christ is a life to celebrate. It all starts with activating God's word. As I apply

God's principles in the Gospel of John, I will learn to pray with streams of living water within my heart produced by the Supreme Being.

- I want to allow Jesus Christ to live through me. Transforming power will do the work. Christianity is the indwelling of God into our everyday activities. I celebrate Jesus for the power flowing within me.

- I want to communicate God to man. Belief gives the authority to place us into his family. I celebrate Jesus for communicating truth to me.

- I am developing a relationship with God through Jesus Crist. Quiet times of meditation have produced the way. I celebrate Jesus for complete sufficiency.

- I want to characterize Jesus. Internal change is taking place. Spiritual transformation is a new part of life. I celebrate Jesus for transformation through the sustainer.
- I am learning to worship with the Spirit of truth. Worship involves love, time choice, sensitivity, and God-consciousness. I celebrate Jesus for giving me the opportunity to worship from the heart.
- I am responsible to respond. It all starts with belief. It involves faith. I celebrate Jesus for saving me from judgement and wrath.
- I am grateful that I have been chosen. I have been enslaved to sin. God has enabled me to believe. I celebrate Jesus for giving me the gift of faith.

- I have been in the center of interpersonal tension. This has included growing in grace. I am yielded to divine control. I celebrate Jesus for helping me to be a peacemaker in conflict. I am thankful for who is in charge of justice. The word salvation means savior. I celebrate Jesus for deliverance and victory over sin and weakness.
- I am thankful for Jesus Christ's credentials. Many people ignore the evidence, causing them to decide to follow their own will
- I celebrate Jesus that he is the light. Blindness is sad. Let God open the blindness to truth. I have a full and free life. Abundance belongs to me through faith. I celebrate Jesus for abundance.

- I see everyday emotion accompanied with sadness, anger, joy, sorrow, hate, love. Feelings are important. I celebrate Jesus for my reliance upon God's sensitivity.
- I am glad to praise God. I love the word "hallelujah". It has brought comfort, hope, love, etc. I celebrate Jesus through the privilege to praise.
- I have learned that love is a permanent badge of discipline and a foundation of unity. Love is submissiveness, active, and constant. I want to infect others with the love of Jesus. I celebrate Jesus for his unconditional love. Genuine love is produced through the indwelling of the Holy Ghost.
- I have been comforted. Jesus jas been the way, truth, and life. I live

with hope. I celebrate Jesus for comfort during suffering. I only have Jesus for comfort during suffering. I only have to apply the previous chapters.

- I have been experiencing remaining in Jesus. Loving Jesus will energize obedience to his commands. I celebrate Jesus as I present my spirit, soul, and body to Jesus. It has to take place in that order.
- I have a helper. The Holy Spirit makes intercession for me. I celebrate Jesus because I can pray to him. Prayer should be and become our first and natural response to every circumstance of life.
- I live in difficult days. Denial could be easy to admit for we

live in a "me-ism" day. I celebrate
Jesus and affirm his promises.

- I am thankful that my sinful
nature has been judged in the
death of Christ. Jesus' resurrection
provides divine enablement. I
celebrate Jesus that my new nature
is developmental.

- I have received the best of … God
has given himself. He gave himself
in Jesus. His love is sovereign. I
celebrate Jesus, that His love will
absorb me and infuse love into
me.

Personal Response

CHAPTER SEVEN

What is the enablement of faith?

he enablement of faith is found in God's provision. Salvation itself is a relation between God as a person and the believer as a person. Faith is my decision to respond to God in trust. It is a gift of God (Rom. 6:23) as given by the Holy Spirit. Faith has its foundation in God's grace (Heb.12:2). For by grace are we saved through faith and that not of ourselves, it is the gift of (Eph. 2:8,9, Rom. 4:16).

The Holy Spirit is the enablement. He is called the spirit of God. "Ye are washed, ye are justified in the name of the Lord Jesus, and by the spirit of our God" (I Cor. 6:11). The Holy Spirit does only what God can do. He is the one who applies this redeeming work of the Lord Jesus described as "washed, sanctified, and justified".

The Holy Spirit is the enablement. He is called the Spirit of Life. "There is therefore now no condemnation to them which are in Christ Jesus, who walk not after the flesh but after the Spirit. The law of the Spirit of Life in Christ Jesus made me free from the law of sin and death" (Rom. 8:1,2). The Holy Spirit has introduced life in the place of death, as well as forgiveness and freedom in the place of guilt and bondage.

The Holy Spirit is the enablement. He is called the Spirit of adoption. "We have not received the spirit of bondage again to fear but ye have received the Spirit of adoption. The Holy Spirit bears witness that we are the children of God" (Rom. 8:15-16). The Holy Spirit has supernatural intervention with our (believers) adoption.

The Holy Spirit is the enablement. He is called Spirit of Grace. Covenant and sin belief and sanctification are activated through grace (Heb. 10:28,29). It involves conviction (John 16:8-11). It involves commitment (Rom. 12:1-2). Grace is the foundation.

The Holy Spirit is the enablement. He is called the Spirit of truth. "I will pray to the Father and he shall give you another comforter that he may abide with you forever, even the Spirit of truth" (John 14:16, 17). The Holy Spirit provides inspiration (God breathed), preservation (God's security), exposition (God's explanation). Illumination (God's understanding), authority (God's confidence).

The Holy Spirit is the enablement. He is called "comforter" which is the Holy Spirit "whom the Father will send in my name, he shall teach you all things" (John 14:26). The Holy Spirit is my helper. The Spirit will lead us into God's will.

Personal Response

CHAPTER EIGHT

What are the characteristics of faith?

I dentify your character through faith. Does my daily life practise God's will? The acceptance of God's gift of faith. "Faith cometh by hearing and hearing by the word of God" (Rom 10:19). Faith is a gift of God not of works' (Eph 2:8,9). Faith is not an abstract or impersonal feeling of confidence. It is inseparably related to a person. The acceptance of a gift which is a person. Jesus Christ is trustworthy.

Faith is faith in a person. It is not blind trust. It is based upon that knowledge of Jesus Christ. It is the acceptance of the word of God. It is submission to the word of God that is true. Biblical faith is not restricted to a mental authority. It is an action of obedience. It is the acceptance of intimate fellowship. Faith is the trust of one person in another person. "Believe on the Lord Jesus Christ and thee shalt be saved" (Acts 16:31). Accepting the gift, accepting the person, accepting the word, accepting in fellowship will demonstrate the faith walk.

Personal Response

CHAPTER NINE

What is the challenge of faith?

" esus said, 'love the Lord your God with all your heart and with all your soul and with all your mind. This is the first and greatest commandment" (Matt. 22:37-38).

The Bible is the sole rule of faith and practice. It is the only dependable source of information. The scriptures are the Oracles of GOd. The finite mind is limited to infinite revelation. The only way to understand is through spiritual illumination. Biblical saturation can be secure through daily study of scripture.

We must obey God's command. Believe in Jesus Christ and accept supernatural power. This week's verse is a command. A lawyer asked the question. He was a professional scholar whose specialty was explaining the application of the law; he knew exactly where the messiah was to be born but lacked the faith to accompany the magi to the place where he was. He shared intellectual argument and sincerity. We need to be informed. Respond with knowledge which is information, facts, and skills, showing God's perspective.

Sensitivity is sharing with respect and emotional awareness.

Insight is understanding the subject with deep respect.

"Jesus said" emphasizes His name which means savior. The name was divinely chosen. Jesus is God. Read John

1:1 and let it saturate your inner being. We need to have a union with Him.

"Love Lord" includes relationship, responsibility, loyalty, and affection. It involves faith, knowledge, and abiding. Love can develop into passion. It can be a driving force provided by the Holy Spirit. Lord means master. He is deity, creator, ruler, supreme being.

"All of the heart" is the nucleus of life, the life principle, the source of life. It is the inbreathing of God that gives the heart life. The heart pumps blood throughout the body and provides life.

"Your soul" is in the image of God. Personality, individuality, intellect-mind, understanding, sensibility-emotion, will-devotion.

"Your mind" is grounded in the saturation of Biblical content. The body possesses flesh, bones, nerves, brains, blood, and vital organs. The soul possesses spiritual intellectual capacity.

The unregenerated man refers to the natural man. He regenerated man belongs to God through faith.

Personal Response

CHAPTER TEN

What is the testimony of faith?

earning to live every monet is God's presence requires claiming his promises. In my book "Discovering God's Favor," I have shared God's faithfulness through using Psalm 23 as a foundation for my childhood events that needed a touch from a faithful God. Take time to read it because it will enhance your spiritual growth. I have great benefits in having a relationship with God the Father through his son, Jesus Christ and the guidance of the Holy Spirit. The divine genius is working daily on my behalf.

I am interested in accepting God's provision for unknown issues that come up in my life. I want to share how this Psalm-poem (Psalm 23) has secured the path for me. It starts with authority that can transform the seeking heart. Deity is suddenly facing me. I can handle anything with God alongside me. All his attributes go into action. In my book, I write about his attributes and later I share thoughts about his name. They have become confidence builders. There is no loss of ground when I know in whom I believe. I have a growing intimate relationship. "The Lord is my Shepherd." It is hard to comprehend or believe but I have communication with God my creator-sustainer-redeemer and Lord.

There is no deficiency in my life. He provides the promise, "I shall not be in want." Contentment can settle me. Only he can provide such rest and peace. He is in charge and the controller of all things. The unknown is directed by his hand of mercy. This is only the beginning. I am able to shout and jump with joy because an infinite, holy, self-existent God in whom I have found has provided the way.

The flies and parasites that torment sheep can be found in fear, tension, worry, uncertainty and the unknown for humans. Panic, discontent, agitation, and restlessness do not have to conquer me. I am going to put his provision into action. The scripture says, "Be still and know that I am God" (Ps. 46:10). I have to learn to be quiet. Quietness for some is a way of life. It can be a time to reflect, a time to create, a time to recover, a time to grieve, a time to rejoice or a time to listen to God. I have to put aside the barriers, schedules, outside interruptions and intrusions. Spiritual intimacy is a must. I think activities and the busyness of life have caused me to get off the right track at times. I have to close my eyes and lay down. I reflect in the fact that God the Father chose me in Christ before the foundations of the world (Eph. 1:4). He predestined me to be adopted as his own (v.5). I reflect on the fact that God the Son carried out God's plan of redemption by shedding his blood on the cross. He redeemed me through his blood and provided forgiveness for my sins (v.7). I reflect on the fact that God the Spirit will enable me to respond in faith to God's love and has guaranteed us inheritance (v. 13,14). This reflection brings peace and security. This will help bring freedom from the unknown.

God says, "wait on me- I will renew your strength, don't run and be weary, don't faint but walk in the Spirit" (Isa. 40:31). I know that God will be with me. He is alive and present whether I feel his presence or not. He will not abandon me. He says "wait on me". I have to rely on him and look to him for my source of strength. Psalm 23 provides what I need to succeed. I do not have to carry the burden of the unknown. God says, give me your burdens, tell me about them, give me your worries and concerns. When I do, I am like the eagle (Isa. 40:31). As he floats effortlessly in the wind, I can do the same because the unknown is placed into God's hands. I am able to experience rest as I reflect upon the God in whom I believe. I must affirm daily that:

- I believe in one and only God and that he is a personal and perfect Spirit who is infinite.

- I believe his attributes describe him and that he is sovereign.
- I believe he will provide rest in the green pasture because he cares.
- I believe in one God who is a trinity and is co-equal, God the Father, God the Son, and God the Holy Spirit, and all three are present with me.
- I believe that God has a plan for all creation and is carrying out that plan. He will provide strength for my part.
- I believe there are no surprises with God. He is carrying out His will through providence.
- I believe that Jesus, begotten by the Holy Spirit, is truly God and man.
- I believe that Jesus voluntarily accepted his Father's will and

came to earth in humanity, lived a perfect life as the sacrificial lamb to take upon himself my sin.

- I believe that Hesus' atonement is the way to my acceptance by God and also the defeat of Satan.
- I believe that Jesus' death totally accomplished the ransom for my sin.
- I believe in Jesus' literal physical resurrection. His resurrection guarantees mine. Believing in Jesus assures God's rest for me.
- I believe that the Holy Spirit is involved in all the acts of God.
- I believe that the Holy Spirit was sent to comfort me and give me rest.
- I believe the Holy Spirit is responsible for my regeneration and transformation.

- I believe the Holy Spirit indwells me and illuminates the Scripture to me.
- I believe that through the Holy Spirit I am able to affirm these facts that will provide rest for my spirit, soul, and body.

As I learn to be in a resting mode, my mind and heart will hold on to the truth of God's Word. My thirst is quenched through his Word. As I allow it to saturate my mind, my soul becomes relaxed with his presence. His thoughts take control of my spirit. It starts with my spirit, then enters my soul, and finally takes charge of my body. I have to learn to disallow the pollution of evil to enter my mind as I drink. The Scriptures will become my measuring rod to test everything. My quiet time will become my measuring rod to test everything. My quiet time becomes a restful, reflective and refueling experience. As I drink of the cool waters, it gives refreshing nourishment, I am putting his provisions into action. I can handle unknown issues in my life because God is equipping me through the Holy Spirit.

I am obtaining rest through recognition that God is giving the rest and a sense of well-being. As I affirm who he is and that he is me, he produces the rest. I will follow him beside the quiet waters. I am not going to drink the dirty water that surrounds or creeps into the back door of my mind, but the pure water that flows from his Word. My thirst will be quenched because the Holy Spirit is doing the leading. I live in a confused and sick society. Christ comes quietly and invites me to come to him. He knows my heart, personality and soul. He has the capacity to satisfy. Only the Spirit and life of Christ himself will make me complete.

As my body needs water to stay alive, it also needs the indwelling of the Holy Spirit and life of the Holy Spirit (I Cor. 6:19) to quench my thrust. I cannot see him but his personality and presence are facts. His personality is proved in John 16:13-14. The pronoun "He" is used eight times to refer to the Holy Spirit. He is a real person because he comes, guides, hears, speaks, glorifies, receives, and he shows.

It is hard to handle the unknown but with a counselor and helper like the Holy Spirit, I am able to succeed. To succeed, I have to follow his leadership by the quiet waters. When my heart is touched by him I have to respond. When his words make an impression in my mind, I must act. I have to practice repentance with honesty.

I have to practice trust with loyalty, I have to practice obedience with love.

In my late teens, I wrote a little booklet entitled "A Touch of Heaven on Earth". I believe now, many years later, in the same things I wrote. If I want God's touch, I have to do what he wants. I have to learn daily to be sensitive to the Holy Spirit's presence. I have to stop resisting the Spirit. I have to stop saying no to his guidance. I have to stop refusing to yield to the Word of God as he brings it home to me. I have to be in a constant attitude of yieldedness rather than rebellion. I have to learn to stop sinning against the Spirit. I grieve the Holy Spirit when I break fellowship with him. Unconfessed sin has to be dealt with on a daily basis. I am not dealing with a force or power or influence, but with a person. The Bible says, "as ye have therefore received

Christ Jesus the Lord, so walk ye in him" (Col. 2:6). I received him by faith and the only way victory is obtained is in my dependence upon the Holy Spirit. He dwells in me and my heart has to be emptied of me and filled with Him. The question is, am I dominated by the Holy Spirit or by myself? Having a "touch of heaven" is through meeting certain conditions: stop resisting the Spirit, stop sinning against the Spirit, stop walking in the flesh.

Right at the time I think all is well, it seems everything will fall apart. The enemy knows my weaknesses. He certainly does not want me to bring glory to the Lord Jesus Christ. I cannot let my guard down. I have to realize that a battle is going on. At all times, I have to stand ready with offensive and defensive weapons.

I can face defeat. I can feel cast down. I can be distressed. I may be frustrated and experience helplessness. I can even enter into depression. The struggles can be big in my eyes but not in God's eyes. I have to keep him, I will sink. Let's keep in mind that Jesus is a caring shepherd. In my spiritual dilemma, he doesn't become disgusted or fed up. I have experienced his love, compassion and tender care. He is ready to give reassurances, patience and restoration. In the path of life, there are many dangers. Restoration takes place when I am free of myself. God knows what he is doing with me. He is in charge. I am glad that he is ready to restore my soul.

I am glad God is ready to restore even when I have missed the mark. Sometimes I have forgotten that a battle is going on. As a musician-trumpeter,

I have played "Sound the Battle Cry!" many times. Verse three says, "O Thou God of all, hear us when we call, help us one and all by th grace; when the battle's done and the victory won, may we wear the crown before thy face." It seems suddenly in the midst of a calm, ordered and peaceful life, all the forces of Satan can break loose. He restores me through giving me understanding of the threefold attack. The act of creation is described as follows: "and the Lord God formed man of the dust of the ground breathed into his nostrils the breath of life; and man became a living soul" (Genesis 2:7). The Scripture reveals that the body was made of the dust of the ground, that the spirit came from the breath of God and that the combination produced the soul (Hen. 4:12). Satan's mind works against the spirit, soul, and body of men. Against the body, he brings the temptations of the flesh. Against the soul, he brings the temptation of the world. Against the spirit, he comes himself or through one of his lesser agents.

I am not a casualty in warfare. I can learn the subtle devices of the enemy, the devil. Let me begin with the flesh or body. I am not referring to the soft substance of the living body which covers the bones and is penetrated with blood. The body has a proper use of its every function and is normal, natural, and moral. There is no sin involved or anything in connection with the human body itself. There is a human side apart from divine influence and it is prone to sin and oppose God. The body cannot run the affairs of the spirit and soul. It has to be controlled by the spirit and soul. When my will chooses to allow my body to dictate what it is going to do, then something is wrong. I am to abstain from anything that is in contrast to the principles of God's Word. I have to be so familiar with his Word that I will know what is right and wrong for me to do. It is not a bunch of rules but applied principles. Run from the enemy. The crucifixion of self has to take place. The enemy attacks the soul with the influence of the world. My senses are the focus. Whatever is drawing me away from the will of God is wrong to follow. If it keeps me away from Jesus, something is wrong. I cannot conform to the world's ideas. Conforming to the image of God's Son will show me what it means to not conform to the world.

Faith is the key word to build upon (I John 5:4), a definite turning away from the world "set eternity in the heart" (Eccl. 3:11). Faith is a daily decision to respond to his Word in the correct way. The devil's greatest interest is my spirit. His desire is to keep me from God's guidance. The sins of the body and conformity to the world are terrible in themselves but the denial of God in the heart is unpardonable. Submission to God is absolutely necessary. Resisting comes next and putting on the armor of God will bring deliverance. In leaning on my own understanding (spirit-sin), I will fail to trust in the Lord with my whole heart (soul-sin) and will allow weakness in the body to flourish (flesh-sin). I am on the winning side with restoration bringing victory in the battle.

Like the sheep, I have to keep moving. I learned a long time ago (Isa. 53:6) "All we like sheep have gone astray, we have turned everyone to his own way and the Lord hath laid on him the son of us all".

I like to go my own way but God knows what is the best way to go. Jesus said, "I am the way, the truth and the life" (John 14:6). Another favorite verse is found in Matt. 6:33, "Seek ye first the kingdom of God and his righteousness and all these things will be added unto you". I am like the sheep- blind, habitual and stupid. The little trails I follow become gullies. Turning to "my own way" simply means what I want. I have to learn to follow Jesus. He says, "If any man will follow me, let him deny himself daily"(Mark 8:34). I may at times give a mental assent to the idea but my will doesn't want to follow. This is the pivot point. The decision has to be made. "I will follow" means a rugged life of self-denial and attitude change. I have to deliberately put myself out on behalf of others. I have to be single-minded. I may have to stand alone. I have to learn to take a back seat. Self-determination has to change to dependence. Circumstances of life don't determine my attitude. Gratitude, peace, and joy are seen in every situation.

Learning to cooperate with the Holy Spirit is the major focus. Right thinking will take place, it is necessary. He makes this possible by his own gracious Spirit who is given to those who obey (Acts 5:32). For it is he who works in us both to will and to do of his good pleasure (Phil 2:13).

I think living righteously will produce correct thinking. My decisions have to be made with eternity in mind and his holiness. In verse three it says "path of righteousness" which is a pleasant and peaceful one because it is through God's name that provides his pure grace for the journey. I think following my own righteousness is worthless. It is built upon a self-achieved list of do's and don'ts. Righteous living and right-thinking involves:

- A relationship with God through belief in his Son.
- A realization that death with Christ and being raised with Christ brings newness of life.
- A recognition that God is doing the work on my behalf.
- A responsibility to get clean.
- A required cooperation with the Holy Spirit.
- A replacement of self-will for God's will.
- A removal of disobedience to daily obedience.
- A reminder to practice gratitude, peace, and joy in every situation.
- I have to adjust to God's thinking. Playing Christianity doesn't work.

His path is full of responsibility and rewards.

There are many valleys I have crept through. I have learned to put the previous provisions into actions. Now I can turn to the most intimate part of the Psalm- "the shadow of death." The sheep face dangers of rampaging rivers, avalanches, rock slides, poisonous plants, and predators. I am fortunate to walk in the shadow of the Almighty. Jesus Christ has conquered death. I don't have to be air-lifted out of the situation. In every situation, in every dark trail, in every disappointment, in an eerie distressing dilemma, I walk with the King. Every mountain has its valleys. The walk may be slow but it can be steady with Jesus. Intimate contact with Christ is the key. He says that he is with me. I have to learn to have an attitude of quiet acceptance of every adversity. Through the adversity, I can move to higher ground. My heart is full of thanksgiving when I realize God has given me a rod and staff to comfort me. The rod or club protects me. The rod becomes the extension of my arm. It is a symbol of strength, power, authority in any serious situation. The rod speaks of the Word of God. It implies the authority of Divinity. The staff provides care. The staff is a symbol of concern and compassion. It is an instrument of patience and kindness. The shepherd leans on it. It is a symbol of the Holy Spirit. The Holy Spirit will guide me, teach me, give understanding, give gentle promptings and counsel me. My reinforcement is provided through the Holy Spirit's constant is provided through the Holy Spirit's constant presence and the use of Scripture against the enemy.

This power comes through his guidance, instruction, understanding, and gentle prompting. It is possible when I become intimate with Jesus Christ. Life can be complicated and cluttered. The Scripture calls for simplicity (Eccl 7:29). Cultivating intimacy with the Almighty will involve a change in life routine. In reading my spiritual autobiography, I discover the necessity to stop. The triple career was exciting but too much. The decision was to simplify. Absolute silence has to follow the simplicity (Ps 46:10). I have to make time for God. The picture is stillness, quietness, listening, and waiting before him. This takes discipline but is indispensable if I hope to add depth to my spiritual life and be reinforced. There is no quick fix in becoming intimate with GOd. In my solitude, God does the examining (Ps. 139:1-4; 23-24). I have to do the confessing (I John 1:9). When I get rid of the complications of life, I am able to find a time for silence. In my silence, I am able to listen to God and make the adjustments. This will provide serenity in the soul. All these activities will bring me to complete trust (Pro. 3:5,6). No longer am I preoccupied with working on the details in my life. Unqualified reliance on the living Lord takes place.

My life will have days of gladness and sadness. It will experience delightful days and dark days. I still have a great, sovereign, gracious, and good shepherd who provides for me even in the midst of my enemies. He anoints my head with oil. He cares for the sheep and he cares for me. The overflowing presence of the Holy Spirit is continually overshadowing me. Coping with unknown issues turns into contentment when my conscious thought-life becomes anointed by the Holy Spirit. I can be free from the world's contamination through faith and acceptance. Just as I have asked Christ to come into my life initially, I need to invite the Holy Spirit to come into my mind to monitor my thought life.

God provides all the preparations to help me. He knows ahead of time my needs. I am blessed with the understanding that he is in charge (sovereignty). I am blessed with experiencing his goodness (grace). I am blessed with his love (mercy). I am blessed with his sufficiency (abundance). I am blessed with his resources (filling). These give me reassurance of his greatness, graciousness and goodness directed toward me.

As I learn to rely on God, his goodness and mercy will pursue me and I will always be at home with him. "I will never leave you nor forsake you" (Heb 15:5). I have a privileged position. No matter what comes, my treatment will be with goodness, mercy, and his presence. I may have limited knowledge, understanding, wisdom, and comprehension, but I have an inner witness of the Holy Spirit. He provides confidence as I work through the provision of rest, refreshment, restoration, right-thinking, reinforcement, reassurance, and reliance. No disaster, difficulty, or dilemma will take charge of my spirit, soul, and body. My serenity has its basis on a total reliance on God's ability to do the right thing and the best things in any given situation for me. God's presence involves his promises.

Personal Responce

CHAPTER ELEVEN

Who is the finisher of our faith?

"Let us draw near to him". The troubled heart in part will vanish when I answer the question, "how do I draw near to Jesus to prepare for heaven?" It is through accepting the exercise of faith in Jesus. I like reading God's Word. Sometimes I only read a verse or two at a time. I listen to the impression it makes upon my spirit. My soul reacts with delight and talks to God through prayer. Faith requires thinking and illumination from the Holy Spirit. I need to know the meaning of faith and how to live victoriously with it. It starts with God speaking, "let us run with patience the race that is set before us. Looking unto Jesus the author and finisher of our faith" (Heb 12:1,2). The theme of Hebrews is a solemn warning against the coming short of victory and encouragement to press on in spite of all my difficulties. Faith is the challenge. I remember in my childhood I learned a broad meaning of the word faith—"forsaking all I trust in". I want to build on its meaning. Remember that willful sinning, deliberate, and continued disobedience and failure to judge known sin may result in "falling away". This results in God's judgement with only one purpose in mind- that of correction, not damnation.

I can have victory through faith. Victory implies a battle. Salvation is free, but victory means sacrifice. To win the race requires discipline. To experience victory, I have to understand faith. Conquering faith is what I am interested in. My childhood faith was easy. I took God at His Word. In the uncertainties of my adult life, I have to do the same thing. I believe the unreasonable, impossible, and unexplainable because someone else in whom I have absolute confidence has said it was so. Upon His Word, I believe it without asking any further proof (Heb. 11:1-3).

I accept the truth simply upon the word of someone else and without proof or any other evidence. It is believing what I cannot see, hear. Feel, taste, smell, or understand. It is confidence in another. Who do I trust? My belief in God is based upon the record of His Word. This is backed up by an eternity of faithfulness.

No one who has ever put his trust in Him has ever been lost or disappointed (I John 5:9,10). I think it all goes back to Genesis 1:1. The natural man wants to reason out the origin of the universe and come up with a thousand speculations. The believer rests upon the simple statement of God: "In the beginning, God created the heavens and the earth." God does not stop to explain. He is not obliged to satisfy my curiosity or stoop to satisfy my mental concerns. He is absolute, final, and true. This first verse of the Bible is the first example of faith. If I can believe that He spoke everything into existence and that He has no beginning or end, I can believe anything else He has to say. I can believe all the miracles: that He could become man and be God, that He prepared for my redemption, that His blood can cleanse me, and that He is the author of faith and its authority.

The victory of faith is won through sacrifice. It is a battle and will cause wounds, scars, and disappointments, yet in the end will be a glorious crown of victory. He requires me to surrender for service, to separate myself from the world, to abstain from sinful pleasures, and to refuse to compromise with evil (Rom. 12:2).

I absolutely need to know how to grow in faith since it is the key to living eternally. How do I live victoriously on a daily basis on my route to heaven? I have learned that worship starts the faith process. I must start with the Lamb of God. The foundation is in my salvation in Jesus Christ. He is the giver of faith. He provides direction, guidance, authority, and confidence. Religious activities are not that means. It is through my daily devotion to Him (John 4:23) and relationship development. My worship will take me from present to eternity, and from eternity to unending life with Christ. It will become a Holy Spirit-stimulated vitality. True worship requires me to approach God with my whole person. It is a love for God in gratitude for what He has done. I have to experience an intimate relationship with God. My invisible part, or spirit, must meet with God. My entire being is activated through love (Matt. 22:37-38). To understand faith requires God-consciousness through praying, praising, reading, the Bible, thoughtful meditations, etc. Faith will grow when I make the choice to be sensitive to God's will. I have to practice the presence of God. My union with Jesus Christ will establish a reliant trust and reverent worship.

The faith process starts with worship and will continue with a walk that glorifies Jesus Christ. I have to ask myself the question, "how deep is my fellowship with Jesus?" Developing communion with Jesus Christ begins by recognizing His residence in me. At the same time, my faith will grow because the foundation is sound. The divine genius of the scriptures, the Holy Spirit, is my indwelling helper and counselor. A change has taken place because I have made a confession of faith (Rom. 10:9, 10). With that confession, the Holy Spirit dwells in me (Rom. 8:9). I have a tremendous responsibility: will Christ be magnified in my body? The top priority is always to die to self. Yielding to God's will and dedication to Jesus as Lord is necessary.His indwelling presence is not in my imagination, but the real thing.

The divine transformation will take place when I answer the question, what does it mean to be Christ-centered? Jesus says give me your body and mind. I have to learn to respond to Jesus' demands. He is the dominant influence in my life. Applied Christianity is spiritual transformation. This involves sound doctrine, renewing of the mind, behavioral change, and a willing heart.

The divine transformation will lead to the divine will. God will work His will in me. He is shaping me into the image of His Son. Each day belongs to Him, and I must surrender all to Him. His will is that I understand that the mind controls the body, the will controls the mind, and the Spirit leads the way. I have to learn to just let go of self and let God do it. He will accomplish His will (Rom. 12:1,2).

The faith process involves sincere worship, a surrendered walk, and sacrificial work. My work ethic is based upon eternity. "Work for the night is coming" (John 9:4). This phrase has led the way to many projects. Faith has opened the door. When worship has the proper motivation, it will prepare me to have the correct mindset- Biblical spirituality. When my walk, or behavior, is Christ-centered, it will prepare me to live out what I believe within. The faith process will be reflected in the work God has given me to do. The proclamation of the Word through music, ministry, and mentoring all have been built upon each other. It has been a joyful experience to reflect on His work being accomplished. Victorious faith will continue with a restful spirit in my life as I worship with sincerity, as I walk in surrender, and as I work sacrificially. The Old Testament heroes of faith like Abel, Enoch, and Noah will be my examples. "I will run the race with patience…looking upon Jesus the author and finisher of my faith" (Heb. 2:1-3).

Personal Response

CHAPTER TWELVE

What have you done with faith?

enuine faith is a practice. It is found in God himself. A believer is united to divinity. Search your heart and answer these thoughts:

I. I must accept God's will in my daily activities
My Yeldedness:
1.
2.
3.

II. The basis of faith is the scripture and it is true

My Strength:

    1.

    2.

    3.

III. The conflict is evil and a war

My Victory:

    1.

    2.

    3.

IV. The union is certain

My Relationship:

    1.

    2.

    3.

V. The transformation is growth

My Righteousness:

    1.

    2.

    3.

VI.   The enemy is sin.
      My Conquest:
      1.
      2.
      3.
VII. The challenge is to choose
      spirituality
      My Decision:
      1.
      2.
      3.

Personal Response

Acknowledgements

appreciate all the people that God has used to influence. Many of these thoughts have come to my memory over the last eight five years through sermon notes, lectures, conversations, meditations and reading. I have not knowingly withheld any significant reference from others in my devotional. To the best of my knowledge all statements and information are true and correct and given credit. Everyone I have come in contact with should be given credit. The pastoral health care ministry is a constant source of encouragement.

PASTORAL
HEALTH CARE
MINISTRY

Pastoral Health Care Ministry

Supernatural Solution Part 1-5
Discovering God's Sufficiency
Discovering God's Love
Discovering God's Counsel
Discovering God's Kingdom
Discovering Heart

Divine Dialogue Part 6-10
Glorify God
Dynamic Doer
Satisfying Strength
Discipling Dynamics
Celebrate Christ

Fantastic Favorites Part 11-15
Discovering God's Presence
Discovering God's Grace
Discovering God's Supernatural Activities
Discovering God's Intimacy
Discovering God's Infinite Nature

Digging Deeper Part 16-20
Faith
Death
Grace
Prophecy

www.ingramcontent.com/pod-product-compliance
Lightning Source LLC
Chambersburg PA
CBHW061704120626
46550CB00003B/1079